QUALITY ASSURANCE IN AI:

NAVIGATING THE ETHICAL FRONTIERS AND THE FUTURE HORIZONS

BY

ADIL QAYYUM

Table of Content

Module 1: Introduction

In the rapidly evolving landscape of artificial intelligence, innovation knows no bounds. AI technologies are reshaping industries, influencing decision-making, and even transforming the way we create art and literature. While the possibilities seem limitless, they also raise profound questions about ethics, safety, and reliability.

"Quality Assurance in AI" is your guide to understanding the vital role of quality assurance in the world of artificial intelligence. It takes you on a journey through the ever-expanding horizons of AI, from the fundamentals of quality assurance to the ethical considerations that underpin the development of AI technologies.

As we navigate this complex terrain, we'll uncover how quality assurance professionals serve as the guardians of ethical innovation. They ensure that AI technologies are not only technically advanced but also ethically sound, reliable, and user-centric. In this book, we explore the challenges and opportunities in AI quality assurance, and we look ahead to the future of AI ethics, where quality assurance professionals play a pivotal role in shaping responsible and ethical AI innovations.

1.1. Quality Assurance Fundamentals

Quality Assurance (QA) is a vital discipline that ensures products and services meet predefined standards and fulfill customer expectations. This section will lay the foundation for understanding the core concepts, methodologies, and practices of Quality Assurance.

1.1.1. What is Quality Assurance?

Quality Assurance is the systematic process of maintaining and improving the quality of products and services. It involves the following key components:

Quality Objectives: Defining clear quality objectives and standards that products or services must meet.

Prevention over Inspection: The emphasis is on preventing defects rather than detecting them post-production.

Continuous Improvement: QA involves continuous assessment and improvement of processes to ensure consistent quality.

1.1.2. QA Methodologies

Quality Assurance (QA) encompasses a range of methodologies aimed at ensuring that products or services not only meet but consistently exceed the required standards. Let's delve into each of these methodologies in more detail:

Manual vs. Automated Testing:

Manual testing involves human testers executing test cases to verify the functionality of a product or service. Testers interact with the system as end-users would, identifying issues, and ensuring the product functions as expected. It's effective for exploratory testing and scenarios that require human judgment.

Automated testing, on the other hand, employs software tools to conduct test cases. Test scripts are created to mimic user interactions and validate functionality automatically. This approach is efficient for repetitive tasks, regression testing, and scenarios with large datasets.

When to Choose: The choice between manual and automated testing depends on factors such as the project's complexity, budget, and the need for rapid testing cycles. Complex, long-term projects may benefit from automated testing, while smaller projects with frequently changing requirements may opt for manual testing for its adaptability.

Functional and Non-Functional Testing:

Functional testing focuses on ensuring that the core functions of a product work correctly. It involves testing features, user interactions, and business processes. Testers verify that the product performs as intended, producing the expected results.

Non-functional testing addresses aspects beyond functionality, including:

Performance Testing: Evaluates the system's responsiveness, scalability, and stability under various conditions.
Security Testing: Identifies vulnerabilities and ensures data protection.
User Experience (UX) Testing: Assesses the product's ease of use, accessibility, and overall user satisfaction.

When to Choose: Functional testing is fundamental and performed throughout the development cycle. Non-functional testing is selected based on project requirements. Performance and security testing are crucial for applications handling sensitive data, while UX testing is vital for customer-facing interfaces.

Choosing the Right Approach:

Selecting the appropriate QA approach involves considering project-specific requirements and constraints. These considerations include:

- Project Scope: Determine the project's size, complexity, and goals.
- Budget: Evaluate the financial resources available for testing efforts.
- Timeline: Assess the project's schedule and time constraints.
- Risk Tolerance: Identify potential risks associated with the project.

Based on these factors, a tailored QA strategy is developed. This might include a combination of manual and automated testing, as well as specific non-functional testing efforts to address the unique needs of the project.

When to Choose: The right QA approach is selected at the project's outset, considering the factors mentioned above. Regular reassessment during the project's lifecycle ensures alignment with changing requirements or constraints.

In short, Quality Assurance employs a combination of methodologies to meet the standards required for a product or service. The choice between manual and automated testing, as well as the inclusion of functional and non-functional testing, is guided by the project's specific characteristics and objectives, ensuring a comprehensive and tailored QA strategy.

1.1.3. Tools and Best Practices

Achieving effective Quality Assurance entails a combination of utilizing the right tools, frameworks, and following established industry best practices. Let's break down these components in more detail:

Popular QA Tools:

The foundation of effective QA often relies on leveraging powerful QA tools and frameworks. Some widely recognized tools include Selenium, JUnit, Appium, and many others. These tools enable testers to automate tests, streamline test execution, and enhance the efficiency of the QA process.

Selection Criteria: Knowing when and how to effectively use these tools is paramount. Each tool serves distinct purposes and is suitable for particular testing scenarios. The choice of tools depends on factors such as the technology stack, project requirements, and the level of test automation desired.

QA Standards and Best Practices:

Quality Assurance is not merely about testing; it's about adhering to industry-specific QA standards and embracing best practices. For instance, standards like ISO 9000 provide a framework for maintaining consistent and reliable QA processes. Industry best practices guide QA teams in achieving high-quality outcomes.

Significance: Following QA standards and best practices ensures that your QA processes are aligned with industry expectations. This not only enhances the credibility of your QA efforts but also fosters a culture of quality within the organization.

Test Case Design and Management:

The efficacy of Quality Assurance hinges on the systematic design and management of test cases. This encompasses crafting test plans, creating test scripts, and organizing test cases to ensure thorough test coverage.

Efficiency in Testing: Efficient test case design and management processes facilitate comprehensive testing. Well-structured test cases help in identifying defects and ensuring that the software or product meets the desired quality criteria.

Life-cycle Management: Test cases evolve throughout the project life-cycle. Effective management ensures that they remain relevant, efficient, and in sync with changing project requirements.

Effective Quality Assurance relies on a combination of powerful QA tools and frameworks, adherence to industry standards and best practices, and efficient test case design and management. The key is to use these tools judiciously, ensure compliance with industry standards, and systematically design and manage test cases to achieve the highest levels of quality and reliability.

1.2. Generative AI Basics

Now, let's get into the fascinating world of Generative AI. It's like having a magic wand that creates new things – but instead of rabbits out of hats, it makes data and art!

1.2.1. Generative AI Overview

Generative AI is like having a super creative robot friend. It can create things that look and sound just like the real deal. Imagine you're playing with your robot friend, and you ask it to draw a picture of a cat. It might not be a real cat, but it looks so close that you'll be amazed!

This magical robot can be used in so many cool ways. You can create art, music, or even write stories. It's like having your very own creative genie.

1.2.2. Deep Learning Fundamentals

Okay, to understand how this magic works, we need to talk about something called "deep learning." It's like the brainpower of our robot friend.

Think of it like this: our robot brain is made of tiny neurons, just like your brain. And these neurons are connected in a big network. When we show the robot lots of examples of something, it learns how to create similar things.

For example, if we show it a bunch of pictures of cats, it learns what makes a cat a cat – pointy ears, whiskers, and that furry tail. Our robot brain learns to draw cats, and it can even make new, unique cats that no one has seen before!

1.2.3. Generative Models

Now, let's talk about how our robot creates things. It uses something called "generative models." These are like recipes for making stuff.

Autoencoders: Think of autoencoders as artists who can paint pictures and then erase parts of them, like magic. But they're not just erasing for fun – they're learning to create pictures that look like the originals.

Variational Autoencoders (VAEs): VAEs are like painters who can create variations of the same picture. It's like making multiple versions of a cat painting with slightly different colors and shapes.

Generative Adversarial Networks (GANs): GANs are the cool kids on the block. There are two parts: one makes stuff (like drawing cats), and the other checks how good it is. It's like having an art duel, and the robot becomes an art genius by trying to outdo itself.

And there you have it! Generative AI is like having a creative, artistic friend who can make amazing things. It's all about learning and creating, just like being a little magician with a wand that makes art and data pop out of thin air!

Module 2: QA and AI Integration

In Module 2, we'll explore the seamless integration of Quality Assurance (QA) and Artificial Intelligence (AI). You'll delve into the crucial aspects of testing AI models, the significance of data quality, and the implementation of evaluation metrics. We'll also investigate bias and fairness testing, and how model validation and verification are essential in the world of AI and QA.

2.1. Testing AI Models

Imagine you're responsible for training a language model to provide customer support chat. This model needs to understand and respond to a wide range of customer queries accurately. However, training is just the first step; you must also ensure the model is functioning as expected.

2.1.1. The Need for Testing AI Models

Testing AI models is like ensuring our language model can handle diverse customer queries effectively. AI isn't perfect; it might misunderstand queries or provide incorrect responses. Testing is essential to identify and rectify these issues, guaranteeing optimal performance.

2.1.2. Data Quality for Testing

To test our language model, we require diverse and high-quality data that mirrors real-world customer queries. Quality assurance tools like Selenium, Protractor, and TestCafe can automate the testing process, ensuring that the language model performs as intended across a variety of customer scenarios. Robust data collection and preparation are essential to simulate real-world scenarios.

2.1.3. Evaluation Metrics

We use evaluation metrics to assess the performance of our language model. In the context of our customer support chat, accuracy is crucial – it measures how often the model correctly understands and responds to customer queries. Additionally, metrics like precision, recall, and F1-score are valuable for in-depth analysis, helping identify areas where the model may need improvement.

2.1.4. Bias and Fairness Testing

It's essential to consider bias and fairness in AI models, especially in customer support scenarios where different demographics and cultural backgrounds are involved. Tools like IBM's AI Fairness 360 and Google's What-If Tool can help identify and mitigate biases. Bias testing helps ensure that our language model treats all customers fairly and impartially, regardless of their background.

2.2. Validation and Verification

Now, let's explore the processes of model validation and verification, ensuring our language model is both reliable and robust.

2.2.1. Model Validation

Validation is akin to ensuring our language model's homework is correct. It involves assessing the model's performance on unseen customer queries, which act as a real-world test. This process is crucial for understanding how well our model handles unfamiliar scenarios.

2.2.2. Model Verification

Verification, on the other hand, is about verifying the model's structural integrity and code quality. Tools like TensorFlow Data Validation and TensorFlow Model Analysis assist in verifying that the model architecture and code are well-constructed. This step ensures that our language model is free from hidden bugs or design flaws that might affect its performance.

2.2.3. Continuous Improvement

In the dynamic world of AI and QA, learning and improvement are continuous processes. We continually refine and enhance our language model to adapt to evolving customer needs.

Tools and technologies like TensorFlow, PyTorch, and scikit-learn allow us to update and fine-tune our model based on ongoing feedback and data. Regular model retraining, fine-tuning, and code optimization ensure that our language model remains a reliable and efficient solution for customer support.

Module 3: Building GANs

This is where the real magic happens. It's time to dive deep into the world of Generative Adversarial Networks (GANs) and learn how to create stunning, realistic data. In this module, we will walk through the essential steps of data preparation, building your GAN architecture, and training it to generate mesmerizing output.

3.1. Data Preparation

Before you can start creating magical art with your GAN, you need to prepare the stage. Just like an artist needs a canvas and paints, your GAN requires the right data for training.

3.1.1. Data Collection

Data collection is the first step in the data preparation process. Imagine you're creating a GAN to generate lifelike images of cats. To do this, you need a diverse and well-organized dataset of cat images.

There are various methods for data collection. You can manually curate a dataset by scouring the internet for cat images and downloading them. Alternatively, you might use APIs to fetch data from online sources, or query databases for relevant content. Some popular tools for data collection include web scraping libraries like Beautiful Soup and Scrapy, as well as APIs provided by websites and platforms.

3.1.2. Data Preprocessing

Once you've collected your dataset, it's time for data preprocessing. Think of this as preparing your canvas by stretching it, applying a base coat, and ensuring it's free from imperfections. Data preprocessing involves several crucial tasks:

Handling Duplicates: Duplicates can clutter your dataset and lead to biased training. You need to identify and remove duplicate data points to ensure data diversity.

Missing Data: Incomplete or missing data can cause issues during training. You might need to handle missing values by filling them in or removing the affected data points.

Uniformity: For GANs to work effectively, your data needs to be uniform in terms of format, size, and quality. For image data, this can mean resizing images to a consistent dimension, standardizing color formats, and normalizing pixel values.

Data preprocessing is often performed using libraries like NumPy and pandas, which offer powerful data manipulation tools. For image data, OpenCV is a popular choice for tasks like resizing, color conversion, and pixel manipulation.

3.1.3. Data Augmentation

Data augmentation is like adding texture and depth to your canvas. It increases the diversity of your dataset and enables your GAN to generate more creative and varied output.

Consider you're training a GAN to create unique cat images. To improve its creativity, you can apply data augmentation techniques, such as:

Rotation: Rotating images by various degrees to present different angles.

Flipping: Creating mirror images to enhance symmetry.

Brightness Adjustments: Tweaking the brightness or contrast to generate images with different lighting conditions.

Data augmentation helps your GAN adapt to a broader range of situations and produce more realistic, captivating output. Deep learning frameworks like TensorFlow and Keras provide data augmentation tools to efficiently apply these transformations to your dataset.

3.2. Building and Training GANs

Creating and training a Generative Adversarial Network (GAN) is where the real excitement begins. This is the stage where you breathe life into your artistic AI model and witness its capacity to generate stunning, lifelike data. Below, we provide a step-by-step guide to help you navigate the process successfully.

3.2.1. GAN Architecture

The architecture of your GAN serves as the blueprint for your artistic masterpiece. Understanding and designing it effectively are crucial to the success of your GAN project. A GAN consists of two key components: the generator and the discriminator.

Generator: The generator is like the creative mind of the artist. It starts with random noise and transforms it into data that resembles your training data. The architecture typically involves layers of neural networks, including convolutional layers followed by upsampling layers.

Discriminator: The discriminator plays the role of the art critic. It evaluates the data it receives, determining whether it's real or generated. Similar to the generator, the discriminator utilizes neural networks with convolutional layers. The design of the discriminator is vital, as it affects the GAN's ability to produce convincing output.

Step-by-Step Guide to Building the GAN Architecture:

Define the Generator: Choose the architecture for your generator. This typically involves specifying the number of layers, the type of layers (e.g., convolutional or dense), and the activation functions (e.g., ReLU or Leaky ReLU). You can use deep learning frameworks like Keras or PyTorch to build the generator network.

Define the Discriminator: Design the architecture for your discriminator. Similar to the generator, you'll determine the number of layers, the layer types, and the activation functions. The discriminator should be capable of distinguishing between real and generated data.

Define Loss Functions: Select appropriate loss functions for both the generator and discriminator. The generator aims to minimize its loss, while the discriminator aims to maximize its loss. The choice of loss functions is crucial for training the GAN effectively.

Optimization Algorithm: Choose an optimization algorithm, such as Adam or RMSprop, to update the model's parameters during training. This step ensures that the generator and discriminator are learning effectively.

Compile the Model: Using the deep learning framework of your choice, compile the GAN model. This involves specifying the loss functions, the optimizer, and any metrics you want to track during training.

3.2.2. Training Process

Training your GAN is akin to honing your artistic skills. It's the phase where you teach your GAN to generate output that is virtually indistinguishable from real data. The training process involves several critical steps:

Data Feeding:

During training, you provide your GAN with two types of data: real data from your dataset and generated data produced by the generator. The generator's aim is to produce data that is as realistic as possible, while the discriminator's goal is to discern real data from generated data.

Training Loop:

The training process occurs in a loop, comprising multiple iterations or epochs. In each iteration, the GAN alternates between two phases: generator training and discriminator training.

Step-by-Step Guide to Training your GAN:

Initialize Model Weights: Before starting training, initialize the weights of the generator and discriminator. This can be done randomly or using pre-trained weights from other models.

Data Preparation: Ensure that your training data is properly formatted and loaded into the model. You may need to apply preprocessing steps, such as normalizing pixel values for image data.

Training Loop:

Generator Training: During this phase, you generate new data using the current generator. The generator's loss is computed based on how well the discriminator can distinguish its output from real data.

Use backpropagation to update the generator's weights and improve its ability to generate convincing data.

Discriminator Training: The discriminator's role is to assess both real and generated data and provide feedback. Its loss is computed to encourage accurate classification of real and generated data. Use backpropagation to update the discriminator's weights.

Repeat: The generator and discriminator training steps are repeated for a set number of iterations (epochs) or until a desired level of performance is achieved.

Monitor Progress: Track the loss functions and evaluation metrics (e.g., accuracy) to monitor the GAN's progress during training. This allows you to identify when the GAN has achieved a satisfying level of performance.

Save the Model: Once your GAN has been successfully trained, save the model weights and architecture. This enables you to use the trained GAN to generate new data in real-world applications.

3.2.3. Hyperparameter Tuning

Just like an artist adjusting colors and brush strokes to perfect their artwork, you can fine-tune hyperparameters to optimize your GAN's performance and output quality. Hyperparameter tuning is an iterative process aimed at improving the GAN's effectiveness and ability to generate convincing data.

Step-by-Step Guide to Hyperparameter Tuning:

Identify Key Hyperparameters: Begin by identifying the hyperparameters that are critical for GAN training. These include learning rate, batch size, architectural choices (e.g., the number of layers), and activation functions.

Initial Parameter Selection: Choose initial values for these hyperparameters based on common practices and guidelines. These initial values will serve as a starting point for optimization.

Perform Experiments: Create a systematic plan for experimentation. This may involve trying different combinations of hyperparameters. For example, you can experiment with various learning rates or batch sizes.

Monitoring and Evaluation: During experimentation, closely monitor the GAN's training progress. Track loss functions, accuracy, and generated output quality. Note the hyperparameter settings for each experiment.

Evaluation Metrics: Determine specific evaluation metrics to assess the GAN's performance. Metrics like Inception Score, Frechet Inception Distance (FID), or perceptual similarity metrics can provide valuable insights into the quality of the generated data.

Comparative Analysis: Compare the results of different experiments to identify which hyperparameter settings yield the best performance. You can create a performance ranking based on your chosen evaluation metrics.

Iterative Refinement: Based on the comparative analysis, refine hyperparameter values. Make incremental adjustments to improve the GAN's performance. This process may require several iterations.

Validation Set: Use a validation set to test hyperparameter configurations that have shown promise. This allows you to validate the improvements in performance before applying them to your GAN.

By following these steps, you can systematically optimize your GAN's hyperparameters, resulting in a GAN that excels at generating high-quality data.

3.2.4. Debugging and Troubleshooting

Artistic masterpieces often come with challenges, and the same is true for GANs. During the training process, you may encounter issues such as mode collapse (where the GAN produces limited variations of data), vanishing gradients (slow convergence), or training instability.

Step-by-Step Guide to Debugging and Troubleshooting:

Mode Collapse: If your GAN is suffering from mode collapse, where it generates the same or very similar outputs repeatedly, try increasing the complexity of the model, modifying the loss functions, or using techniques like mini-batch discrimination to encourage diversity in generated data.

Vanishing Gradients: To address vanishing gradients, which result in slow convergence, you can experiment with different activation functions (e.g., Leaky ReLU), adjust learning rates, and explore advanced optimization algorithms like RMSprop or Adam.

Training Instability: If your GAN's training is unstable, where it exhibits sudden performance drops or erratic behavior, you can experiment with gradient penalties, implement gradient clipping to limit extreme updates, and increase the batch size for more stable updates.

Monitoring Loss Functions: Continuously monitor your GAN's loss functions. Significant fluctuations or anomalies in loss curves can indicate training instability or convergence issues.

Early Stopping: Implement early stopping strategies to halt training if your GAN's performance is degrading. This can save time and computational resources when it's clear that further training won't improve results.

Regularization Techniques: Explore regularization techniques like weight decay or dropout to prevent over-fitting and enhance the generalization of your GAN.

Visualization Tools: Utilize visualization tools to gain insights into the GAN's training process. Visualization can help you identify issues and make informed adjustments.

By effectively debugging and troubleshooting your GAN, you'll be better equipped to overcome challenges and produce stunning, lifelike data.

3.2.5. Continuous Improvement

Just as artists continually refine their techniques to create better art, the training of GANs is an ongoing process. To ensure your GAN consistently generates captivating data, you can implement continuous improvement strategies.

Step-by-Step Guide to Continuous Improvement:

Regular Retraining: Periodically retrain your GAN using updated datasets and optimized hyperparameters. This ensures your GAN remains relevant and adapts to changing data distributions.

Feedback Loop: Establish a feedback loop with real-world users or applications that utilize the generated data. Collect feedback and iteratively improve your GAN based on user preferences and needs.

Model Ensembling: Explore model ensembling, where you combine the outputs of multiple GANs to enhance the diversity and quality of generated data.

Advanced Architectures: Stay up to date with advancements in GAN architectures. Experiment with cutting-edge architectures and techniques to push the boundaries of what your GAN can generate.

Ethical Considerations: Continuously evaluate the ethical implications of the data generated by your GAN. Ensure it adheres to ethical guidelines and fairness standards.

By following these steps, you can ensure your GAN remains a powerful tool for generating data that meets the highest quality standards.

Module 4: Quality Assurance and Testing of GAN Projects

This module is all about ensuring the quality of your Generative Adversarial Network (GAN) projects, leveraging the power of generative AI for testing and validation. Here, we dive into the critical realm of quality assurance and testing in the context of GANs and generative AI.

4.1. Quality Assurance through Testing

In the realm of GAN projects and generative AI, quality assurance (QA) is paramount. The quality of the generated data not only influences the success of your project but also has real-world implications. In this section, we'll explore comprehensive techniques and strategies to ensure the highest quality of generated data through rigorous testing and validation.

4.1.1. Data Validation and Testing

Data quality is the cornerstone of reliable GAN-generated data. By thoroughly validating and testing the data, you can minimize errors and inconsistencies, ensuring the GAN's output meets the highest standards.

Technique 1: Data Collection

Data collection is the foundation of your GAN project. It's essential to be meticulous and thoughtful when sourcing your data:

Data Source Diversity: Ensure your dataset comprises diverse examples. For instance, if you're training a GAN to generate human faces, include images of various ages, ethnicities, and expressions.

Relevance to Objective: Align your dataset with the specific goals of your project. If you aim to generate realistic landscapes, a dataset of landscapes from different regions and climates is critical.
Data Enrichment: You can enhance data quality by enriching it with metadata, labels, or annotations that describe the content, location, or other relevant attributes.

Technique 2: Data Preprocessing

Data preprocessing is the step that ensures your data is clean and ready for testing and training. It involves a series of operations to prepare the data for maximum quality:

Duplicate Removal: Identify and eliminate duplicate data points. For instance, if your dataset contains multiple copies of the same image, these should be removed to prevent overrepresentation.
Handling Missing Data: Determine how to address missing data points. For textual data, you might choose to impute missing values with common words, while for images, you may opt to discard incomplete data.
Uniformity and Consistency: Ensure uniformity in data format, dimension, and units. If you're working with images, standardize the image dimensions, color schemes, and pixel values.

Technique 3: Data Augmentation

Data augmentation techniques enhance the diversity of your dataset, which, in turn, can lead to higher-quality GAN-generated data. Consider these strategies:

Image Data Augmentation: For image data, use techniques such as rotations, flips, brightness adjustments, cropping, and scaling. For example, if you're generating images of animals, augment the dataset by rotating images to simulate different angles.
Text Data Augmentation: In text data, introduce variety by paraphrasing sentences, inserting synonyms, or generating similar

but unique sentences. This will ensure a broader spectrum of text for your GAN to learn from.

4.1.2. Performance Testing

Performance testing evaluates how effectively the GAN generates data under various conditions. By rigorously assessing performance, you can optimize your GAN for high-quality output.

Technique 1: Load Testing

Load testing simulates various user demands and evaluates the GAN's response. It is crucial to ensure that the GAN can meet performance expectations:

Load Scenarios: Create load scenarios that mirror real-world usage. For example, if your GAN generates text, simulate different levels of concurrent text generation requests.
Response Time Analysis: Measure response times under various loads. Analyze how the GAN's performance changes as the demand increases. This analysis can help identify bottlenecks and areas for improvement.

Technique 2: Stress Testing

Stress testing pushes the GAN to its limits, helping identify weaknesses and potential points of failure:

Maximum Load Testing: Apply the maximum expected load to the GAN to determine its breaking points. If, for example, you're generating high-resolution images, stress the GAN with large volumes of image requests.
Resource Utilization Monitoring: While stress testing, closely monitor the GAN's resource utilization. Pay attention to memory

consumption, CPU, and GPU usage. Anomalous resource utilization can signal potential performance degradation.

Technique 3: Endurance Testing

Endurance testing ensures that the GAN maintains consistent performance over extended periods, which is vital for applications requiring continuous data generation:

Prolonged Testing: Run the GAN continuously over an extended duration, such as 24 hours or more, to assess its long-term performance and identify any potential memory leaks or degradation over time.
Resource Leakage Assessment: While conducting endurance testing, focus on resource leakage. Monitor memory usage and the GAN's resource allocation to uncover resource management issues that may affect prolonged performance.

4.1.3. Validation and Verification

Validation and verification are essential steps to ensure that the GAN-generated data aligns with project requirements and that the GAN operates as intended. These processes safeguard data quality and reliability.

Technique 1: Model Validation

Model validation evaluates the quality and appropriateness of the data generated by the GAN. It ensures that the GAN produces output that meets project objectives:

Quality Metrics: Define specific quality metrics tailored to your project. For instance, if you're generating images, metrics like structural similarity (SSIM) and peak signal-to-noise ratio (PSNR) can assess image quality.

Data Comparison: Compare the generated data to real-world examples to verify that it matches the characteristics, patterns, and attributes of genuine data. This can be achieved through visual inspection, quantitative metrics, or both.

Stakeholder Feedback: Gather feedback from project stakeholders, end-users, or domain experts. Their input is invaluable for validating that the generated data is suitable for the intended use and aligns with their expectations.

Technique 2: Model Verification

Model verification focuses on confirming that the GAN's code, structure, and functionality align with the project's design and objectives. It ensures that the GAN behaves as expected:

Code Review: Conduct a comprehensive code review to verify that the GAN's implementation adheres to design specifications and project requirements. Pay attention to coding standards, documentation, and adherence to best practices.

Functional Testing: Thoroughly test the GAN's functions to ensure that it operates as intended. This may involve assessing input-output relationships, algorithm behavior, and the integration of the GAN with other components of your project.

Performance Assessment: Measure the GAN's performance to verify that it meets predefined standards for speed, accuracy, and resource utilization. Performance testing, as discussed earlier, can also be part of the verification process.

Best Practices for Quality Assurance through Testing

To ensure the highest quality of GAN-generated data, consider the following best practices:

Establish Testing Protocols: Define clear testing protocols and procedures to ensure consistency and repeatability in your testing efforts. Document these procedures for reference and future use.

Test Data Diversity: Ensure that your testing data is as diverse as your training data. This diversity should encompass variations in content, style, and any other relevant attributes.

Automation: Implement automation wherever possible in your testing processes. Automated testing tools can save time and ensure thorough and consistent testing.

Scalability Testing: If your project is expected to scale, assess how your GAN performs under increased load. Scalability testing is crucial to ensure that your GAN can meet growing demands.

Real-World Simulation: Whenever feasible, simulate real-world scenarios in your testing. This can involve using actual data, traffic patterns, or user behaviors to assess the GAN's performance in a lifelike context.

Collaboration: Involve stakeholders, domain experts, and end-users in your testing and validation processes. Their feedback and insights are invaluable in ensuring that the GAN meets real-world requirements.

Regular Updates: Continuously review and update your testing and quality assurance procedures. Stay informed about advancements in GAN technology and adapt your processes accordingly.

Documentation: Thoroughly document your testing processes, results, and any issues encountered. This documentation not only helps in addressing immediate concerns but also aids in long-term quality improvement.

Ethical Considerations: Always consider the ethical implications of your GAN-generated data. Ensure that the data adheres to ethical guidelines and fairness standards.

By following these techniques and best practices, you can effectively ensure the highest quality and reliability of GAN-generated data through comprehensive testing, validation, and verification. Rigorous quality assurance processes are essential for the successful deployment of generative AI projects in real-world applications, from healthcare to art, and from manufacturing to entertainment. The quality of the data generated by your GAN is a reflection of the care and precision applied throughout the development process.

4.2. Practical GAN Quality Assurance Projects

The Practical GAN Quality Assurance Projects section provides a hands-on opportunity to apply quality assurance techniques to GAN-generated data. In this section, we'll explore in-depth strategies and best practices for assessing and ensuring the quality and reliability of GAN output in various domains.

4.2.1. Quality Assessment of Image Generation

Image generation is one of the most compelling applications of GANs. Ensuring the quality of generated images is paramount, and here we will delve into techniques and best practices for image quality assessment.

Technique 1: Image Evaluation Metrics

Measuring the quality of generated images requires a set of objective metrics that can quantitatively assess factors like image sharpness, color fidelity, and overall quality. Some commonly used metrics include:

Structural Similarity Index (SSIM): SSIM measures the structural similarity between the generated image and the ground truth. It considers luminance, contrast, and structure, providing a value between -1 and 1, where 1 indicates a perfect match.

Peak Signal-to-Noise Ratio (PSNR): PSNR calculates the ratio between the maximum possible power of the image and the power of noise. Higher PSNR values indicate higher image quality.

Inception Score: Inception Score measures the quality and diversity of generated images. It considers both the realism and diversity of the generated samples.

Frechet Inception Distance (FID): FID assesses the quality of generated images by comparing feature representations of the generated and real data. A lower FID indicates closer similarity between the two datasets.

Technique 2: Testing Image Diversity

Image diversity is a critical aspect of image generation. The GAN should be capable of producing a wide variety of images, rather than repeating the same patterns. To ensure image diversity:

Visual Inspection: Conduct visual inspection of the generated images to verify that they cover a broad spectrum of styles, content, and characteristics. Pay attention to variations in color, texture, and structure.

Data Stratification: Stratify the generated images to assess whether they match the characteristics and distribution of the training data.

This helps identify any biases or deficiencies in the generated dataset.

Semantic Understanding: Use semantic understanding techniques to categorize and analyze the generated images based on their content. Ensure that the GAN produces images with semantic diversity.

4.2.2. Text Generation Validation

Text generation projects require validation to ensure that the generated text is coherent, contextually appropriate, and adheres to the desired style. We'll explore techniques to validate text quality.

Technique 1: Text Coherence Testing

Coherence is a critical aspect of text quality. Coherent text is logical, flows well, and is easy to understand. To assess text coherence:

Language Models: Use language models, like GPT-3, to evaluate the coherence of generated text. These models can provide a quantitative measure of how well the generated text follows the context.

Cohesion Metrics: Cohesion metrics analyze how well sentences and paragraphs connect with each other. Metrics like the Flesch-Kincaid readability score can provide insights into text cohesion.

Real-World Context: Compare the generated text to real-world examples or reference texts. Ensure that the generated text is contextually appropriate and maintains coherence.

Technique 2: Validation with Real-World Data

Validating text generation quality involves comparing the generated text to real-world examples to ensure accuracy and appropriateness:

Real-World Comparison: Collect a set of real-world text data that aligns with the context and style of the generated text. Use this real-world data as a reference for validation.

Contextual Relevance: Assess how well the generated text fits into the context of the task. Verify that it provides information or responses that are contextually relevant.

Domain-Specific Evaluation: In domain-specific applications, ensure that the generated text meets domain-specific requirements and terminology.

4.2.3. Artistic Style Transfer Verification

Artistic style transfer is a creative application of GANs, where one image's style is applied to another. To ensure the quality and fidelity of style transfer, consider the following techniques:

Technique 1: Visual Style Validation

Visual style validation assesses the quality of style-transferred images by measuring their visual appeal, consistency, and artistic fidelity. Some key aspects to consider include:

Visual Quality Metrics: Employ image quality metrics like SSIM and PSNR to measure the visual fidelity of style-transferred images. A high SSIM indicates similarity to the original image.

Artistic Style Preservation: Ensure that the artistic style of the source image is faithfully transferred to the target image. This involves retaining the key visual elements and characteristics of the style.

Content-Style Balance: Evaluate the balance between content and style in the transferred image. The content should be clear, and the style should be pronounced but not overwhelming.

Technique 2: Comparing Style Transfer

Comparing style-transferred images with the original source and target images is essential to confirm the success of style transfer. Here's how to approach it:

Visual Comparison: Visually inspect the style-transferred image alongside the original source and target images. Look for similarities in stylistic elements, such as brush strokes or color schemes.

Fidelity Metrics: Use metrics that assess the fidelity of style transfer, such as feature map comparisons or deep neural network-based metrics.

Preference Testing: Consider conducting preference testing with human evaluators who can assess the artistic quality and faithfulness of style transfer. This qualitative feedback can be invaluable.

4.2.4. Peer Review and Feedback

As a final step in the Practical GAN Quality Assurance Projects section, peer review and feedback provide a valuable opportunity for collaborative evaluation. It's an essential practice for learning, sharing insights, and evaluating the quality assurance strategies employed in your GAN projects.

Technique 1: Peer Review Sessions

Organize peer review sessions where learners and participants in the course assess and provide feedback on each other's GAN projects. These sessions can be conducted in person or virtually, and they serve several purposes:

Knowledge Sharing: Participants can learn from one another, gaining insights into various quality assurance strategies and best practices used in different GAN projects.

Feedback Gathering: Peers can evaluate the quality of the GAN-generated data and provide constructive feedback. This feedback may focus on aspects such as image clarity, text coherence, or style transfer fidelity.

Benchmarking: By comparing your GAN project's performance with those of peers, you can identify strengths and areas for improvement, enhancing the overall quality assurance process.

Technique 2: Expert Consultation and Feedback

Incorporate the expertise of mentors or instructors who are well-versed in the field of generative AI and quality assurance. Their guidance and feedback can be invaluable for fine-tuning your GAN project's quality assurance processes:

Expert Assessment: Experienced instructors or mentors can provide expert assessments of the quality of your GAN-generated data. They can offer insights into the strengths and weaknesses of your approach.

Quality Improvement Recommendations: Experts can suggest specific improvements to enhance the quality and reliability of your GAN project. These recommendations may cover data preprocessing techniques, model fine-tuning, and testing strategies.

Domain-Specific Insights: For domain-specific GAN projects, mentors can offer insights into the unique challenges and considerations related to quality assurance within that domain. This domain expertise can be critical for achieving high-quality output.

Technique 3: Collaborative Feedback

Encourage collaborative feedback within your peer group. Learners and participants can provide insights, suggestions, and constructive criticism based on their own experiences and perspectives:

Quality Evaluation: Collaborative feedback allows participants to collectively assess the quality of each other's GAN projects. They can evaluate the clarity, coherence, and artistic fidelity of images, text, or style-transferred content.

Discussion Forums: Create discussion forums or platforms where participants can share their GAN projects and request feedback from the community. This open dialogue fosters a collaborative learning environment.

Quality Assurance Best Practices: Share best practices related to quality assurance and testing within the course community. Participants can exchange ideas and strategies for improving the quality of GAN-generated data.

By actively engaging in peer review, expert consultation, and collaborative feedback, participants in the course can benefit from diverse perspectives, learn from one another's projects, and enhance the quality assurance of their GAN-generated data.

Quality assurance in GAN projects is an ongoing process that involves iterative testing, validation, and feedback. As learners progress through the Practical GAN Quality Assurance Projects section, they will refine their skills in assessing and ensuring the quality and reliability of GAN-generated data. This hands-on experience is essential for preparing them to apply their knowledge in real-world scenarios, where high-quality GAN output is a prerequisite for success.

Module 5: Shaping the Future of QA and AI

We now explore crucial aspects influencing the AI landscape, with a focus on the necessity of proper quality assurance.

5.1. Ethical AI: Ensuring Quality and Fairness

In the realm of AI, ethical considerations have taken center stage. As we navigate this advanced topic, we'll explore the nuances of ethical AI and the crucial role of quality assurance in ensuring that AI systems are not only technologically advanced but also fair, just, and aligned with human values.

5.1.1: Ethical AI Fundamentals

Let's delve into the fundamental aspects of ethical AI, supported by practical examples that illustrate the significance of quality assurance.

Understanding Ethical AI with Practical Insight:

In our rapidly evolving digital world, AI is a ubiquitous presence, influencing various facets of life. Consider the deployment of AI algorithms in recruiting processes. A company relies on an AI system to shortlist candidates for job interviews. The AI, trained on historical data, inadvertently learns biases present in the data. This results in the AI system disproportionately selecting candidates from certain demographic groups while neglecting others. This scenario exemplifies the ethical dimensions of AI: the potential for bias, discrimination, and unfairness. Quality assurance in AI is the safeguard that should have been in place to detect and rectify such biases before they influence decision-making.

AI Bias and Fairness - A Quality Assurance Imperative:

AI systems, especially those employing machine learning, rely heavily on data for their decision-making. However, this dependence on data carries the risk of bias seeping into the AI's algorithms. A real-world case in point is the use of AI in the criminal justice system. Predictive policing tools, powered by AI, analyze crime data to predict future criminal activity. These tools have faced criticism for reinforcing bias, as they can perpetuate the over-policing of certain neighborhoods. Quality assurance must be incorporated at each stage of AI development to scrutinize and mitigate such bias. It involves meticulous data analysis and algorithmic fairness checks. Ethical AI development insists on this kind of quality assurance to ensure fairness and equity.

Data Privacy and Quality Assurance - A Moral Imperative:

Data privacy is another ethical pillar underpinning AI development. Consider a healthcare organization that employs AI to analyze patient records and provide diagnostic insights. The sensitive nature of healthcare data mandates rigorous data privacy safeguards. Quality assurance, in this context, entails stringent data protection measures. Quality assurance experts validate that AI systems adhere to stringent data anonymization and encryption protocols, ensuring the utmost privacy and compliance with regulatory standards. Failure in ensuring data privacy can result in legal and ethical repercussions.

The Transparency and Accountability Nexus - A Prerequisite for Ethical AI:

Transparency in AI systems is essential for establishing trust and accountability. Let's take the example of autonomous vehicles. These self-driving cars rely on AI algorithms to make real-time decisions. In the event of an accident involving an autonomous vehicle, accountability becomes a critical concern. Quality assurance processes are designed to ensure transparency in the decision-making of AI systems. Engineers and quality assurance professionals demand that AI systems provide explanations for their actions. This is especially important in high-stakes situations such as autonomous vehicles, medical diagnostics, and financial algorithms. Transparency is the path to accountability, and quality assurance is the guardian of this transparency.

5.1.2: AI in Society - Shaping a Quality-Driven Future

Here we explore how AI applications in critical sectors like healthcare, criminal justice, and employment underscore the importance of quality assurance for ethical AI implementation.

AI in Healthcare - Quality Assurance for Patient Well-being:

The application of AI in healthcare holds immense promise, but it also presents ethical challenges. Consider an AI system designed to assist radiologists in identifying cancerous lesions in medical images. Quality assurance plays a pivotal role in ensuring the accuracy of these AI-driven diagnoses. Radiologists and quality assurance experts collaborate to rigorously validate the AI system's outputs. Quality assurance checks verify that the AI system's accuracy aligns with human standards. Failure to maintain this high level of quality assurance can have dire consequences for patient well-being, as incorrect diagnoses could lead to delayed treatments or misdiagnoses.

AI in Criminal Justice - Quality Assurance and Fairness in Legal Decisions:

In the realm of criminal justice, AI is employed for various purposes, including risk assessment and sentencing. An illustrative example is the use of AI algorithms to predict the likelihood of recidivism among individuals on parole. The ethical concerns are profound, as these predictions can have direct consequences on individuals' lives. Quality assurance in AI for criminal justice is indispensable for validating the fairness and accuracy of risk assessment tools. Quality assurance experts collaborate with legal experts to assess the tool's effectiveness in predicting recidivism and ensure it is unbiased. Quality assurance is the cornerstone for justice and fairness in AI-assisted legal decisions.

AI in Employment - Navigating Workforce Transformations:

The introduction of AI in the workplace brings significant changes. AI-driven automation can enhance efficiency but can also displace human workers. Quality assurance practices play a pivotal role in this context. Imagine a company introducing AI-driven automation for routine tasks. Quality assurance professionals are responsible for validating the system's accuracy, efficiency, and impact on the workforce. Their role extends beyond the technical realm; it includes assessing the ethical implications of workforce displacement. Quality assurance, in this context, becomes the driving force for ethical employment practices and the protection of workers' rights.

As AI continues to permeate various sectors, the role of quality assurance in upholding ethical standards becomes increasingly crucial. Practical examples vividly illustrate how quality assurance is not a mere technical procedure but a moral and ethical imperative. Quality assurance professionals become the guardians of fairness, equity, and justice in AI, ensuring that AI technologies are ethical, reliable, and aligned with human values.

5.2. Future Trends: Quality Assurance in the Evolving AI Ecosystem

The future of artificial intelligence is a captivating realm that promises innovations and advancements in various domains. As AI technologies continue to push boundaries, the role of quality assurance becomes increasingly pivotal. In this section, we delve into the exciting future trends of AI, underlining the necessity of robust quality assurance to ensure ethical, reliable, and innovative AI ecosystems.

5.2.1: The Next Frontier in Generative AI - Quality Assurance for Creativity and Innovation

Here we explore emerging trends in generative AI that have the potential to revolutionize creativity and innovation. At the heart of these trends is the need for quality assurance to ensure that AI-driven creativity aligns with ethical and artistic values.

AI-Enhanced Creativity - The Role of Quality Assurance

As AI becomes an integral part of the creative process for artists, writers, and creators, it opens new avenues for innovation. AI tools can generate music, art, and literature, assisting creators in their endeavors. These AI-generated creations can be awe-inspiring, but they also raise questions about their ethical and artistic value.

Consider a scenario where an artist employs AI to create digital artwork. The AI, driven by generative algorithms, produces stunning visuals. These creations blur the line between human and machine-generated art. Quality assurance in AI-enhanced creativity extends beyond technical assessments. It encompasses ethical and artistic evaluations.

Quality assurance professionals collaborate with artists to ensure that AI-generated art adheres to ethical principles and aligns with the artist's intentions. They meticulously review the artwork to confirm that it retains its artistic authenticity. This quality assurance process is not just a technicality; it's an ethical commitment to ensure that AI contributes to creative excellence without compromising ethics.

AI-Generated Content - Ensuring Quality and Originality

The creation of content by AI is a transformative trend that impacts journalism, marketing, and various content-based industries. AI algorithms can generate articles, music, and even realistic images, raising questions about the quality, originality, and ethical integrity of such content.

Consider a newsroom that employs AI to generate news articles. AI-driven content creation can significantly boost the efficiency of news production. However, it also raises ethical questions regarding the accuracy and authenticity of the content. Quality assurance in this context becomes indispensable for upholding journalistic ethics and the reliability of news.

Quality assurance experts scrutinize AI-generated content to ensure accuracy, originality, and adherence to ethical standards. They assess whether the content aligns with the newsroom's integrity and editorial policies. The quality assurance process acts as a gatekeeper, preventing the dissemination of false or misleading information. It becomes the ethical vanguard that ensures AI-generated content maintains high standards, contributing positively to journalism, marketing, and other content-driven fields.

AI in Design and Architecture - Quality Assurance for Transformation

AI's influence on design and architecture is profound. AI algorithms can optimize building designs for energy efficiency, enhance urban planning, and generate innovative architectural designs. This trend presents new frontiers for quality assurance, as safety, functionality, and compliance with industry standards become paramount.

Imagine an architectural firm that employs AI to optimize structural designs for a new skyscraper. AI-driven algorithms can fine-tune the design for maximum stability and energy efficiency. However, quality assurance experts are tasked with ensuring that these AI-generated designs not only meet safety standards but also align with ethical and sustainability principles.

Quality assurance professionals conduct rigorous assessments of AI-generated architectural plans to validate safety, structural integrity, and compliance with ethical and environmental standards. They work in close collaboration with architects and urban planners to ensure that AI contributes to innovative and sustainable designs while upholding the highest ethical and safety standards.

In summary, this subsection highlights the pivotal role of quality assurance in upcoming trends in generative AI. It showcases quality assurance as the guardian of ethical creativity, original content, and innovative designs, ensuring that AI-driven innovations align with ethical principles and human values.

5.2.2: Ethical Considerations in Future AI - Quality Assurance as a Safeguard

This section anticipates ethical challenges in the ever-evolving AI landscape and emphasizes the role of quality assurance in providing safeguards. As AI continues to advance, quality assurance becomes the gatekeeper for ethical AI applications and emerging technologies.

AI and Deepfakes - The Imperative of Quality Assurance

Deepfake technology has emerged as a potent force in the digital landscape. It involves the manipulation of audio and video to create highly convincing but entirely fabricated content. The potential for deepfakes to spread misinformation, facilitate identity theft, and invade privacy raises profound ethical concerns.

Quality assurance professionals play a pivotal role in developing tools and techniques to detect and counter deepfakes. Their work is a testament to the evolving landscape of quality assurance, which extends beyond traditional testing and validation. In the case of deepfakes, quality assurance experts employ AI-driven algorithms to scrutinize media content for signs of manipulation.

The quality assurance process in this context involves training AI models to recognize anomalies in media content. It includes identifying inconsistencies in facial expressions, audio patterns, and even the source of media content. By doing so, quality assurance becomes the guardian of trust and authenticity in a world increasingly inundated with digital media. It ensures that society can rely on the authenticity of audio and video content, safeguarding against the deceptive potential of deepfakes.

AI in Autonomous Systems - Quality Assurance for Safety and Accountability

Autonomous systems, including self-driving cars and drones, represent a prominent trend in the AI landscape. These systems rely on AI algorithms to make real-time decisions, with safety as the utmost priority. As autonomous systems become more integrated into daily life, quality assurance becomes a fundamental safeguard for their ethical and reliable operation.

In the case of autonomous vehicles, quality assurance plays a crucial role in ensuring that AI algorithms make safe and ethical decisions. Quality assurance experts conduct rigorous testing to validate the accuracy of perception systems, the reliability of decision-making algorithms, and the overall safety of autonomous vehicles.

Consider a self-driving car navigating a complex urban environment. Quality assurance professionals are tasked with validating that the AI algorithms can accurately recognize pedestrians, obey traffic laws, and make ethically sound decisions in challenging scenarios. The quality assurance process is not just a technical procedure; it's a moral imperative that safeguards the lives and well-being of individuals.

AI and Super-intelligent Systems - Ensuring Ethical and Quality-Driven Development

The development of super-intelligent AI systems, often referred to as artificial general intelligence (AGI), presents unique ethical challenges. AGI systems have the potential to surpass human capabilities, raising questions about control, ethics, and the consequences of their actions.

Quality assurance in this context is multifaceted and far-reaching. Quality assurance experts work alongside AI developers to ensure that super-intelligent systems are developed in a manner that aligns with ethical principles and human values. This involves rigorous testing and validation of the systems' decision-making processes.

Imagine a scenario where an AGI system is designed to assist in complex decision-making, such as medical diagnoses or environmental policy recommendations. Quality assurance professionals collaborate with domain experts to assess the accuracy and ethical soundness of the AGI system's recommendations.

The quality assurance process extends beyond technical assessments to encompass the ethical and societal impact of AGI. Quality assurance experts play a critical role in ensuring that AGI systems prioritize safety, ethics, and accountability. Their work becomes an ethical cornerstone in the development of super-intelligent AI, safeguarding against unintended consequences and ethical dilemmas.

Quality Assurance in the Evolving AI Ecosystem

Quality assurance in AI is not a static concept; it evolves alongside AI technologies and their applications. The traditional role of quality assurance in software and product development is now augmented by ethical considerations, safety protocols, and societal impact assessments. In the evolving AI ecosystem, quality assurance has several dimensions:

Technical Validation: Traditional quality assurance involves rigorous testing, validation, and verification of AI algorithms and systems. This process ensures that AI applications function correctly and reliably. Quality assurance experts conduct testing to identify and rectify technical errors, ensuring the robustness of AI systems.

Ethical Auditing: Ethical considerations have become integral to quality assurance in AI. Quality assurance professionals assess AI algorithms for bias, fairness, and compliance with ethical standards. Ethical auditing involves evaluating how AI decisions impact different demographic groups and ensuring that AI systems do not discriminate.

Transparency Assessment: Quality assurance experts validate the transparency of AI systems. This involves assessing whether AI systems can provide explanations for their decisions. Transparency is essential for accountability and understanding how AI reaches specific conclusions.

Privacy Validation: Quality assurance extends to privacy assessments, particularly in AI applications that involve user data. Quality assurance experts ensure that AI systems handle data ethically, respecting user privacy and complying with data protection regulations.

Safety and Reliability Checks: In AI applications like autonomous systems, quality assurance focuses on safety and reliability. Experts verify that AI-driven systems are safe for operation, have fail-safes in place, and adhere to ethical safety standards.

Performance Optimization: Quality assurance includes performance optimization. Experts fine-tune AI algorithms to improve efficiency, accuracy, and response times. This aspect is crucial in various AI applications, from recommendation systems to medical diagnostics.

Adaptability Testing: Quality assurance also evaluates AI systems' adaptability to changing circumstances. This is essential in AI applications that need to respond to dynamic environments, such as self-driving cars that must navigate unpredictable traffic scenarios.

Compliance Assessment: In regulated industries, quality assurance ensures that AI systems comply with legal and industry-specific standards. Experts validate that AI applications meet the necessary compliance requirements, such as those in healthcare, finance, or aviation.

The evolving landscape of quality assurance in AI is characterized by a broader scope that encompasses not only technical validation but also ethical, safety, and societal considerations. Quality assurance professionals play a pivotal role in upholding the ethical and reliable development of AI technologies, ensuring that they align with human values and societal expectations.

Challenges and Opportunities in Quality Assurance for AI

In the realm of Quality Assurance for AI, the ever-evolving landscape offers a multitude of challenges and opportunities for professionals in the field. Let's explore these challenges and opportunities in greater detail:

Challenges:

AI Bias and Fairness:

- Identifying Bias: Recognizing bias in AI algorithms and models that may result in discriminatory outcomes.
- Mitigation Strategies: Developing techniques to address bias and ensure fairness in AI decision-making processes.

Data Privacy:

- Regulatory Compliance: Navigating a complex web of data protection regulations (e.g., GDPR) while handling vast datasets.
- Robust Data Protection: Implementing comprehensive measures to safeguard data privacy, including anonymization, encryption, and access control.

Complexity of AI Algorithms:

- Deep Learning Complexity: Understanding and testing complex AI algorithms, particularly those based on deep learning and neural networks.
- Transparency and Accountability: Ensuring the transparency and accountability of AI algorithms to enhance their trustworthiness.

Evolving Regulations:

- Regulatory Awareness: Keeping up-to-date with constantly evolving AI-related regulations, standards, and ethical frameworks.
- Adaptation and Compliance: Adapting quality assurance practices to comply with new regulations and standards as they emerge.

Opportunities:

Ethical Advancements:

- Ethical AI Advocacy: Quality assurance professionals have a unique opportunity to advocate for ethical AI development.
- Ethical Guidelines: Shaping AI technologies to align with ethical principles and human values, promoting responsible AI deployment.

Innovation in Safety Protocols:

- Safety-Critical AI: Pioneering innovative safety protocols in AI, particularly in critical areas like healthcare and autonomous systems.
- Fail-Safe Mechanisms: Developing and testing fail-safe mechanisms to enhance the ethical use of AI in applications where safety is paramount.

User-Centric Innovation:

- Enhanced User Experience: Embracing a user-centric approach to innovation, leading to more user-friendly, intuitive, and effective AI applications.
- Usability and Accessibility: Focusing on ensuring that AI technologies cater to a diverse range of users, including those with disabilities.

Trust and Acceptance:

- Building Trust: Quality assurance practices contribute significantly to building trust in AI technologies.
- Adoption Enabler: Trust is a cornerstone for the widespread adoption of AI, and quality assurance plays a pivotal role in establishing and maintaining that trust.

Future Directions for Quality Assurance in AI

As AI technologies continue to advance, quality assurance should adapt to these changes and take on new roles that are essential for the future of AI. The directions that quality assurance should explore include:

AI Ethics Integration: Collaborating with AI ethics experts, quality assurance professionals should integrate ethical considerations into their processes, ensuring that AI technologies not only function well but also adhere to ethical standards.

AI Bias Mitigation: Quality assurance experts should play a central role in the development and implementation of advanced techniques for detecting and mitigating bias in AI systems.

Privacy-Centric Quality Assurance: Quality assurance should evolve to focus more on data privacy, including implementing robust data protection measures, conducting privacy audits, and assessing compliance with privacy regulations.

AI Transparency Standards: Quality assurance professionals should contribute to establishing standards for AI transparency, working to make AI systems capable of providing clear and understandable explanations for their decisions.

Regulatory Compliance Expertise: As AI regulations evolve, quality assurance experts should specialize in regulatory compliance, ensuring that AI applications conform to both legal and ethical standards.

Cross-Domain Quality Assurance: Quality assurance should expand its scope to cover various industries, with experts specializing in domains such as healthcare, finance, or automotive, ensuring adherence to industry-specific standards.

AI Validation at Scale: With AI systems handling increasingly complex tasks, quality assurance processes should adapt to validate AI technologies at a larger and more sophisticated scale.

In the coming years, quality assurance in AI will remain an ever-evolving field, rising to meet the complexities and challenges posed by advancing AI technologies. Quality assurance professionals will serve as ethical compasses, reliability gatekeepers, and innovation enablers within the dynamic AI landscape.

In summary, quality assurance is not a hindrance to AI innovation; rather, it is a catalyst for ethical, reliable, and user-centric advancements in AI. As AI continues to reshape industries and society, quality assurance stands as a fundamental pillar, ensuring that AI evolves responsibly and ethically, in line with the highest standards of human values and societal expectations. This adaptability is crucial for quality assurance to remain relevant and effective in the evolving AI ecosystem.

www.ingramcontent.com/pod-product-compliance
Lightning Source LLC
Chambersburg PA
CBHW062258290526
45794CB00006B/2611